Malmesh

Probably the book J. ... read !

Ashtavakra Gita
Dialogues with King Janak
Direct, Simple, Easy to Understand

****

Raj Doctor is an architect, town-planner, management expert.
He has worked with and headed several international
not-for-profit and social organisations.
He has already authored a novel *'Melancholy of Innocence' (2011)*
Currently he lives in Amsterdam and Jaipur. This is his first non-fiction literary work.

****

To Amrut
[Nectar]
My Dad

Only after he passed away I realized:
"How deep he LOVED me...."

****

Assertion is Violent, Philosophy is self-indulgent, Morality is Pseudo, Rights are Imposed Burden,
Identification an Illusion, Authoring a verbal dysentery, and Work - destructive struggle against nature.

The Author negates the self-indulging pseudo burden of any illusions life's struggle may leave on mind & nature.

Introduction

Ashtavakra Gita is written as a dialogue between sage Ashtavakra and Janaka, king of the kingdom Mithila. *Ashtavakra Gita*, is advaitic[1] masterpiece stating the whole truth without duality un-like Bhagawat Gita that was recited much later by Lord Krishna to his charioteer warrior Arjun and which serves varying interpretation for everyone who reads it. Nothing is known about the first author of *Ashtavakra Gita*, but there are various Sanskrit versions and English translation available with commentary.

Human mind - much evolved; yet cannot stop itself from adding new interpretations to existing completeness of things around it.

Asthavakra Gita is such a case in text; interpreted from its basic Sanskrit form by scholars and gurus – each one adding one's own pretension as their scholarly interpretation.

The truth to be understood is: the more commentary and explanation one tries to give to the text of *Ashtavakra Gita*, the more it takes the readers away from the essence of *Ashtavakra Gita*.

For me, there is no denial in believing that the basic text of *Asthavakra Gita* in Sanskrit was 'not' tempered. I strongly think that before any translations was done to any other language, the Sanskrit text was changed; mostly, misrepresented by Sanskrit religious scholars to bring some meaning by unscrupulous simplification by adding degenerating to the original text.

I have been reading various versions of *Asthavakra Gita* since 1990s in different languages. Since then, the more I have studied *Asthavakra Gita*, the more I have realized – **one**, the quality of poor translations - most authors are missing the core essence, from Sanskrit to Sanskrit and later from Sanskrit to English and **second**, the *useless* additions (the second line) to the already existing completeness (of first line). Why should one add words when brevity does communicate? The more I read it the more I realized that how fractured the translations must be from the basic Sanskrit text. The currently available Sanskrit text in itself has that duality of addition of second line, the duality *Ashtavakra Gita* wants us to deny.

---

[1] *Advaitic means Non-dual, (Not two)*

Most additions – especially the second line in each verse / couplet in the Sanskrit text made me smile at the *farness* of extreme opposite meaning the available original text communicates to its readers. An example to illustrate this is how often *'be happy'* is used as an ending text in the second line of many verses and couplets (by those who have tempered with its original text) forgetting that *being happy* is an emotion like any other emotion that *Ashtavakra* tells us to discard – then how come one continuously keeps on saying *be happy* again and again!?

One example illustrates this:

The translation of **|| 1-2-2 ||** as done by one author goes like this,

If you are seeking liberation my son,
Avoid the object of senses like poison
And cultivate tolerance, sincerity, compassion,
contentment and truthfulness as the antidote.

While another author has translated like this:

To be free,
Shun the experience of senses like poison
Turn your attention to
Forgiveness, sincerity, kindness, simplicity and truth.

After understanding *Ashtavakra Geeta's* true message and essence, I understand and believe the first two lines are sufficient to express the core point, and I strongly think that the other two lines are much later additions by scholars through many centuries or millennia in trying to explain the unknown "next" and thereby missing out on the core essence and understanding of *Asthavakra Gita* in its fullness. It is a snare that so called learned Sanskrit scholars could not resist interpreting and showcasing to the world their half-knowledge.

How my interpretation could be or is different? I have simplified the text for everyone to understand. I have removed those burdens of second lines from the original text and left the core meaning as it is:

If you are seeking liberation
Shun the subject of consciousness like poison || 1-2-2 ||

There is no need to add those second lines because it takes away the realness of what the original text is meant to say. Instead the second line gives a direction that human beings are always looking for on *"What to do?"* thus I have removed the same. It tries to give another additional interpretation to what *Ashtavakra Gita* could had intended to tell us; I believe *Ashtavakra Gita* does not want us to fall in the trap of following a path, a direction, a dictum, a morale, a self righteous way, but wants us to dwell simply in the inner seeking.

My intention is to weed out the **"unnecessary"** from the original Sanskrit text. What I present here is the basic text – which I feel communicates the real zest of original *Asthavakra Gita*.

If you require more words to understand Asthavakra Gita, you will not understand it at all, anytime soon.

Another important thing to note is that King Janak to whom the discourse is shared is also very knowledgeable king, but his knowledge is like most intelligent humans – like a half filled bucket that spills more than needed with unnecessary words and jargons – that is how King Janak shows off his little knowledge in front of *Ashtavakra*.

To many readers the words of King Janak may also seem enlightened, but King Janak knows that what he knows is not complete and that is why Ashtavakra is called for a dialogue to complete, clarify and simplify King Janak's knowledge.

It is *Ashtavakra* who builds upon King Janak's understanding and brings total clarity.

The chapter that is the most important in capturing the essence of *Ashtavakra* – is chapter *eighteen*; where *Ashtavakra* opens up the knowledge of universe to King Janaka, which King Janaka happily repeats by negating the existence in the last two chapters. Try to read and understand them more intently.

Remember, the enlightenment within *Asthavakra Gita* does not lie in spoken or written words.

**"The less said and more understood with fewer words,
the better the understanding."**

The beauty of *Asthavakra Gita* is this: the moment one tries to explain it with analogies, descriptions, images, metaphors and similes; one looses the real meaning of *Ashtavakra Gita*. Don't fall into those decoys.

For completeness of *Ashtavakra Gita* – explanation is a baggage. If you read or listen to anything extra to understand *Ashtavakra Gita*, you will carry the burden of the explanation and get confused. It may seem you have understood, but in reality any type of explanation has already pushed you far away from the core essence of *Ashtavakra Gita*.

Once you understand this pitfall - and after that if you will read or listen to any translation and explanation of Ashtavakra – you will know the futility of words and you will smile at the commentator, scholar, teacher or guru who is trying to explain *Ashtavakra Gita*.

Another important thing one should keep in mind is – do not try to practice things identified as virtues of wise, intelligent and liberated person, because putting effort in believing and practicing those things is in itself going against the fundamental grain of teaching of *Ashtavakra Gita*.

Delve into the essence, make it your being!

Raj Doctor
January 2015

|| The Beginning ||

|| Thus *The Asthavakra Gita* begins ||

DAILOGUE BEGINS

HOW TO ATTAIN KNOWLEDGE?

|| Chapter One ||

Janak said ||

How to get knowledge?
How to know more on subject of liberation? || 1-1-1 ||

Asthavakra said ||

If you are seeking liberation
Shun the subject of consciousness like poison || 1-2-2 ||

There is no earth, no water,
No air nor ether || 1-3-3 ||

The body-like consciousness
Restfully observe it || 1-4-4 ||

You do not belong to any different class
Nor you are what you perceive yourself to be || 1-5-5 ||

Your acts and actions, pleasure and pain
Do not belong to your self. Know that || 1-6-6 ||

Remain a witness to everything
And remain free always || 1-7-7 ||

You have falsely believed in the untruth of
"I am the BIG doer" || 1-8-8 ||

This one impure lesson of 'self'
Now decide to burn it || 1-9-9 ||

Whatever appears in the universe
Is like an imagined mountain of ropes || 1-10-10 ||

Priding oneself as liberated, one feels liberated
Similarly, priding oneself as bound, one feels bound || 1-11-11 ||

Stand to witness your self
To complete the action of liberating oneself || 1-12-12 ||

Firmly learn the lesson of
Un-limited consciousness without any duality || 1-13-13 ||

You are priding your identity with body
Tear of that binding, dear || 1-14-14 ||

Be without any bindings and actions,
And be self illuminating and pure || 1-15-15 ||

You are the entire universe
The universe is there 'as it is' within you || 1-16-16 ||

Remain neutral, formless,
And fearless like water || 1-17-17 ||

Whichever has form, or can get a form
Decide to reject it || 1-18-18 ||

Be the mirror reflecting within itself
The beauty of things around it || 1-19-19 ||

The same air and space exist
Outside and within all forms || 1-20-20 ||

JANAK'S UNDERSTANDING OF
STATE OF REALIZATION

|| Chapter Two ||

Janak said | |

Oh Pure soul I understand that,
The lesson of peace is different from nature | | 2-1-21 | |

Only because of light alone
We can see this body and the world | | 2-2-22 | |

I realize abandoning the love
Of body and world | | 2-3-23 | |

Like waves, foam and bubble
Are no different from water | | 2-4-24 | |

To think of threads
Not being part of cloth is not possible | | 2-5-25 | |

Similarly, juice from sugarcane
Is always sweet like sugar | | 2-6-26 | |

From knowledge of self one realizes the world
One cannot realize the world without self-knowledge | | 2-7-27 | |

Light is my only nature
But I am nothing more than this form of light | | 2-8-28 | |

Oh, this distorted knowledge of world
Is because of my ignorance | | 2-9-29 | |

The universe that emanated from my perception
Will also dissolve within me | | 2-10-30 | |

Oh, I bow myself
Even in destruction of world, I will not die | | 2-11-31 | |

Oh, I bow to myself
Even I am ONE soul within my body| | 2-12-32 | |

Oh, I bow to myself
There is no one as powerful as me | | 2-13-33 | |

Oh, I bow to myself
I who possess nothing of this world | | 2-14-34 | |

Knowledge, knowable and knower – all three
Does not exist in reality | | 2-15-35 | |

Searching for duality and differences is
The root cause of misery || 2-16-36 ||

This lesson itself is my only knowledge
Every other qualification is imagined by myself || 2-17-37 ||

I am neither bounded nor liberated
That illusion of peace has ceased || 2-18-38 ||

This body and the universe
Is without form or substance is certainty || 2-19-39 ||

Body, heaven, hell, bondage, liberation,
and fear too is imagination || 2-20-40 ||

Oh, even among the crowd of people
I do not find any difference or duality || 2-21-41 ||

I am not body, nor I have a living body
Nor I am consciousness || 2-22-42 ||

Oh, universe making sound, strange images
Comes into my consciousness and inner memories || 2-23-43 ||

Inside me, like infinite big ark of consciousness
There is light || 2-24-44 ||

Inside me, like infinite big ark of consciousness
To my wonder my mind is puzzled || 2-25-45 ||

ASHTAVAKRA'S EXPLANATION OF SEEKER'S STEP

|| Chapter Three ||

Asthavakra said ||

You have indestructible soul
That is the one thing you have realized|| 3-1-46 ||

Knowledge of self
That subject itself has lead you to illusionary perceptions || 3-2-47 ||

The world's energy cycle
Are like continuous waves in the ocean || 3-3-48 ||

On hearing of pure consciousness
Your soul will become beautiful || 3-4-49 ||

Every being is within your Self
Your self is in every being|| 3-5-50 ||

This state of supreme lesson
Is perfect for liberation || 3-6-51 ||

Wonderful knowledge
Is rare to get in company of bad friendship || 3-7-52 ||

This learning has de-generated into
You believing in this and that self righteous behaviors || 3-8-53 ||

The one who feeds on tranquility
Is never ever tormented || 3-9-54 ||

This eagerly desiring body of yours
See it as someone else's body || 3-10-55 ||

Universe is in between various illusions
Everything else is just a subject of curiosity || 3-11-56 ||

You think you are a desire less person
Or a disappointed saint || 3-12-57 ||

But while perceiving the nature of things
You know that what one you see is by its very nature 'nothing' || 3-13-58 ||

Be unattached, beyond dual opposites
And free from seeking any blessings || 3-14-59 ||

JANAK'S UNDERSTANDING OF SEEKER'S EXPERIENCE

|| Chapter Four ||

Janak said ||

One who has self-knowledge
Plays the game of desirous life || 4-1-60 ||

Every day, this is the state
All the Gods yearn for... || 4-2-61 ||

For this type of enlightened person
Virtue or vice does not touch anytime || 4-3-62 ||

One who has knowledge of universal non-destroyable soul
Is a great soul || 4-4-63 ||

In this illusionary world of ghostly villages
There are four beings || 4-5-64 ||

One who lives within self, one who identifies with other communities
One who acts without fear, one who considers themselves as GOD || 4-6-65 ||

ASHTAVAKRA'S EXPLANATION ON NATURE OF UNIVERSE

|| Chapter Five ||

Asthavakra said | |

What do you want to renounce?
Put the complexity to rest, you are PURE as you are || 5-1-66 ||

The whole universe arises from you
Like bubbles out of the sea || 5-2-67 ||

Everything present in the world
Is unreal and manifested by you|| 5-3-68 ||

You are complete in your happiness and pain
You are equal in hope and despair || 5-4-69 ||

JANAK'S UNDERSTANDING OF
MY REAL KNOWLEDGE

|| Chapter Six ||

Janak said ||

I am the infinite space of the sky within a jar
In this natural world || 6-1-70 ||

I am like the shore-less ocean
And all the universal things are like waves || 6-2-71 ||

I am the mother of all pearls
And the illusionary world is the silver reflecting on it || 6-3-72 ||

I am in all being
And all beings are in me || 6-4-73 ||

JANAK'S UNDERSTANDING OF PRACTICAL LIFE AND KNOWLEDGE

|| Chapter Seven ||

Janak said | |

Within the infinite ocean of my mind
The world drifts from here and there | | 7-1-74 | |

Within the infinite ocean of my mind
That is the nature of the universe | | 7-2-75 | |

Within the infinite ocean of my mind
The so called world is ill-imagined | | 7-3-76 | |

My soul is not in emotions
Nor my emotions are in the infinite and spotless soul | | 7-4-77 | |

Oh, a little bit of it is a wonder
Otherwise the world is like a magician's show | | 7-5-78 | |

ASHTAVAKRA'S EXPLANATION ON BONDAGE AND LIBERATION

|| Chapter Eight ||

Ashtavakra said ||

Wherever there is bondage there is worry
Why are you longing and grieving about useless things || 8-1-79 ||

Whenever you will get liberated from these worries
You will not grieve, nor will you long || 8-2-80 ||

Wherever there is bondage there is worry
This has made you see distorted imaginations || 8-3-81 ||

Whenever there is no 'me', there is liberation
Otherwise there is always bondage || 8-4-82 ||

ASHTAVAKRA'S EXPLANATION ON DETACHMENT

|| Chapter Nine ||

Ashtavakra said | |

Your doing - un-doing and duality of things
For whom have they given peace? | | 9-1-83 | |

Those are the blessed one who don't live
According to other people's expectations and observations | | 9-2-84 | |

Certainly without any doubt, all other declarations'
Has lead you to misery of your essence of understanding things | | 9-3-85 | |

Was there any age of time,
That we did not face duality and differences any time? | | 9-4-86 | |

There is no agreement between
Seers, saints and experts of meditation | | 9-5-87 | |

You yourself will see knowledge away from those idols
And develop fully evolved consciousness and not your teacher | | 9-6-88 | |

After giving existence to the forms and being,
Whereas you have been seeing only forms and beings | | 9-7-89 | |

There is lust and the worldly society everywhere
Be without those forms and beings | | 9-8-90 | |

ASHTAVAKRA'S EXPLANATION ON PEACE

|| Chapter Ten ||

Ashtavakra said | |

Be indifferent to everything
Desire and intellect form the circle of your life | | 10-1-91 | |

This dream-like net of existence
Will only last for three to five days | | 10-2-92 | |

Whenever wherever desire occurs in the mind
The evolvement of worldly structure emerges | | 10-3-93 | |

Only the desires of the soul is the bondage
Destruction of it ascends you to liberation | | 10-4-94 | |

Within you there is innocence and pureness
Whereas the world is non-existent | | 10-5-95 | |

Within the Kingdom, within oneself,
Within the body, there is only pleasure | | 10-6-96 | |

For the sake of getting prosperity and desires
Stop doing pious deed | | 10-7-97 | |

Since how many births
Beings are falling into this trap? | | 10-8-98 | |

ASHTAVAKRA'S EXPLAINATION ON WISDOM OF LIFE

|| Chapter Eleven ||

Ashtavakra said ||

This deformity from one emotion to another emotion
There is the certainty of your visiting self-nature || 11-1-99 ||

God is not the creator of all
Learn this with certainty || 11-2-100 ||

In the times of problems and fortunes
Certainly, Gods and Goddesses have exist || 11-3-101 ||

In the times of happiness and sadness
Certainly, Gods and Goddesses have exist || 11-4-102 ||

With awareness gone
Certainly, nothing else but suffering has prevail || 11-5-103 ||

I am not the body, nor is the body in me
Certainly this is the moral lesson || 11-6-104 ||

From the limitless sky to the bottom of the grass roots
Certainly, I am the alone who is existing || 11-7-105 ||

In this non-astonishing world
Certainly, nothings created by self is existing || 11-8-106 ||

JANAK'S UNDERSTANDING OF STEPS LEADING TO WISDOM

|| Chapter Twelve ||

Janak said | |

For supporting any physical actions
We support it with a long deliberation | | 12-1-107 | |

Each emotion we convert it into
Words and images with our mind | | 12-2-108 | |

Mutual acceptance of contrarian situations
That is the behavior we have accepted | | 12-3-109 | |

We reject separations and sorrow
And the subjects of happiness | | 12-4-110 | |

Place of rest or without rest; meditation or self search of consciousness
This should be avoided | | 12-5-111 | |

Performance of actions is due to no-knowledge
So it total inaction | | 12-6-112 | |

Thinking of unthinkable
Is like praying for worries | | 12-7-113 | |

Just like that doing actions and self done actions
I have learnt to differentiate between them | | 12-8-114 | |

JANAK'S UNDERSTANDING OF BLISS

|| Chapter Thirteen ||

Janak said | |

The world without materialistic things
It is difficult to manage oneself healthily | | 13-1-115 | |

The thought of starting prevents one from doing certain thing
And curiosity prevents one of thinking to start | | 13-2-116 | |

No action is ever committed
Always this element of self-thought is there | | 13-3-117 | |

With the emotions of un-doing or not-doing also
Those who meditate are also attached to human body | | 13-4-118 | |

Meaning of right or wrong does not come from this position
Even while walking or sleeping | | 13-5-119 | |

Sleeping and dreaming does not cause any harm
Nor does success and achievements have done any good | | 13-6-120 | |

The rules of pleasures and pain
I have observed these emotions frequently | | 13-7-121 | |

JANAK'S UNDERSTANDING OF BLISS TESTED

|| Chapter Fourteen ||

Janak said | |

One whose nature is empty minded
And unmindfully shows different types of emotions || 14-1-122 ||

Where is wealth? And where are friends?
On my own I have knowledge on different subjects || 14-2-123 ||

Through knowledge and wisdom, in witness of your personal self,
I wish to realize the Supreme soul of Lord || 14-3-124 ||

Carrying the non-existence and end-ness of duality
Can be identified as clean and spotless || 14-4-125 ||

I

ASHTAVAKRA'S EXPLANATION ON
SELF - REALIZATION

|| Chapter Fifteen ||

Ashtavakra said | |

Even after casual teaching lessons
A person can be intelligent by one's own self | | 15-1-126 | |

Detach yourself from the subject of liberation
If you are interested in that subject, then it is your bondage | | 15-2-127 | |

Speaking of this self gained knowledge like a big business enterprise
Makes people dumb and stupid | | 15-3-128 | |

You are not the body, nor is the body yours
Nor you are the doer or reaper of consequence in this world | | 15-4-129 | |

The attitude of blaming everything around you, is the duty of mind
But the mind is not yours, nor ever has been | | 15-5-130 | |

Your soul is in all beings,
All beings are in your soul | | 15-6-131 | |

The world's energy is within you
Just like waves within ocean | | 15-7-132 | |

Have faith in yourself my child
But don't let yourself delude in this love | | 15-8-133 | |

Virtues are invented by your self
Like the existence of body, it comes and goes | | 15-9-134 | |

Let the existence of your body remain till the end of imagination
Or else let its elements perish today and again | | 15-10-135 | |

Let the limitless big ocean within you
Be just like the universal nature | | 15-11-136 | |

Child, within you is pure consciousness
And it is not different from this universe | | 15-12-137 | |

The one within you as a part of you is peace
Just like the infinite limitless sky is within you | | 15-13-138 | |

Anything else you perceive in this world
Immediately you will find its one existence is manifested within you | | 15-14-139 | |

'I am not in everything – this and that'
By yourself discard the distinction of such differentiations | | 15-15-140 | |

Due to your self-ignorance the universe exists,
In reality within you there is absolute meaning of everything || 15-16-141 ||

Just like illusion this world is
Certainly, there is nothing more than that || 15-17-142 ||

Only 'ONE' existed in this world's ocean
Exists and will exist in future || 15-18-143 ||

So don't disturb your mind with decisions and options
Just let your mind shine as pure consciousness || 15-19-144 ||

So give up meditation completely
Do not let your mind hold to anything || 15-20-145 ||

ASHTAVAKRA'S EXPLANATION ON WITNESS

|| Chapter Sixteen ||

Ashtavakra said | |

You may read, listen and recite my child
Countless scriptures and religious books | | 16-1-146 | |

Whatever you indulge in – wealth, any activity or meditation
Those are the ones that will bring obstructions to you | | 16-2-147 | |

Everyone is in pain because of their own self-efforts
Nobody knows this ever | | 16-3-148 | |

Like while purchasing things for business you have
This habit of taking inside and outside view of everything | | 16-4-149 | |

If you avoid this dull behavioral policy
Your mind will always remain free from duality | | 16-5-150 | |

People are witness to subjects where wrong behavior is involved
Remains non-attached to the subject matter | | 16-6-151 | |

So long as you desire
Those are the sprouting roots of worldly affairs | | 16-7-152 | |

If the self done activities will go, all the cause of disease will retire
So will go all your problems | | 16-8-153 | |

One who wants to renounce the world
Remains unhappy in that hope | | 16-9-154 | |

Everyone takes pride in
Loving their efforts of liberation or their beautiful body | | 16-10-155 | |

One who is witness to one's own liberation, is liberated
Let even the lotus be your instructor to this process | | 16-11-156 | |

ASHTAVAKRA'S EXPLANATION ON THE KNOWLEDGE OF TRUTH

|| Chapter Seventeen ||

Ashtavakra said | |

If you are able to attain the fruits of this knowledge
Then only this meditated learning will be successful | | 17-1-157 | |

Even with any elements of important things you come across
The knower of truth is never distressed by any of these elements | | 17-2-158 | |

No subject of any elements attract them
Who has found delightful self peace within their self | | 17-3-159 | |

One who enjoys and has enjoyed things of this world
Does not exist in the elements of this world | | 17-4-160 | |

The world full of 'without any desires'
Looks like an image of 'full with desires' | | 17-5-161 | |

Duty, learning, activity, liberations,
Even birth and death exists here | | 17-6-162 | |

One who does not want dissolution of all these worldly things
Nor does have any aversions towards it – is in the RIGHT state | | 17-7-163 | |

Without defining meaning to actions, or towards different forms of knowledge
Be contended and fulfilled | | 17-8-164 | |

Desire for a non-conforming witnessing
And for inoperative inactive senses | | 17-9-165 | |

Don't be awake, or asleep
Nor keep your eyes open or close | | 17-10-166 | |

The world and self seen from everywhere or whichever side, looks healthy
Looks pure at heart from everywhere | | 17-11-167 | |

There is non-seeing, non-hearing, non-touching, non-smelling,
Non-eating, non-taking, non-speaking, non-walking | | 17-12-168 | |

There are no blames, no praises,
Nor any rejoices or any disappoints | | 17-13-169 | |

There is equitable compatibility and poise seeing the other sex,
And unperturbed with approaching death | | 17-14-170 | |

Man and woman will go through happiness and pain
And may live together and separated | | 17-15-171 | |

There is no violence or compassion

44

Nor there is pride of knowledge or humility or humbleness || 17-16-172 ||

There is no witnessing the subject of liberation
Nor there is attachment to that subject || 17-17-173 ||

Resolution and contemplation
One should not know such alternatives || 17-18-174 ||

Devoid of the feeling of 'I' and 'me'
Knowing with certainty that nothing is || 17-19-175 ||

Is mind free from display of
Gathering of delusions, dreams, ignorance and stubbornness?|| 17-20-176 ||

ASHTAVAKRA'S EXPLANATION ON UNIVERSAL NATURE

|| Chapter Eighteen ||

Ashtavakra said ||

By knowing these lessons
It reveals the world like a dream || 18-1-177 ||

By acquiring playful objects means
One would get all sorts of desired fulfilled || 18-2-178 ||

Sorrow arises out of duty
This scorching sun of sorrow will burn your soul and heart || 18-3-179 ||

The whole existence is just emotions
There is no meaning to things in reality || 18-4-180 ||

Neither far nor limitless
That's the realm of your inner self || 18-5-181 ||

By elimination of your outer longing and delusion
What will remain is your true self nature that is beautiful || 18-6-181 ||

Everything around you is just imagination
And the only truth is that your soul is free || 18-7-182 ||

Certainly, your soul is universal
Different types of emotional behaviors are just imaginations || 18-8-183 ||

'I am this and that' – that is not true
At this very moment, break that imagination || 18-9-184 ||

There are no different opinions, nor there just one agreement
There is no common lesson; there is no ignorance || 18-10-185 ||

Even under your own rule, or even in a beggar's attitude
Even in gain or loss, even among people or in solitude forest || 18-11-186 ||

There is no religious duty, or there is any other work,
Nor there is any different type of knowledge or any courtesy || 18-12-187 ||

Work, there isn't any to be done
Nor there is any attachment within the heart || 18-13-188 ||

There are no desires, or there is any world around you
Nor there is anything like meditation, nor liberation || 18-14-189 ||

Those who will really be witness of what is going in this universe
Will really try to deny every activity within it || 18-15-190 ||

Who witnesses the whole universe within oneself
Develops the universal cosmic energy and soul || 18-16-191 ||

One who witnesses the duality within one's heart
By their own self, will obstruct such dualities | | 18-17-192 | |

Today you stand against people's popular opinion
Tomorrow, in the future – that will be people's popular opinion | | 18-18-193 | |

That one who is without different types of emotions
One who is satisfied and free from any desires | | 18-19-194 | |

Be the one who is - while doing activity or while being inactive
Is always patient to face any calamity | | 18-20-195 | |

Be the one who is without any desires, without any attachments
Is self-reliant and free of any bonds | | 18-21-196 | |

Once you transcend this worldly society
There is no joy nor sorrow | | 18-22-197 | |

One who never desires to kill this curiosity
Nor feels sense of loss in anything | | 18-23-198 | |

One's own nature has reached an empty state of mind
Whatever the one does, it comes out of one's body | | 18-24-199 | |

Whatever activity happens, is done by the body
And not me, that is the pure nature of oneself | | 18-25-200 | |

One who does things without saying 'Why I am doing it'
Is not a child who is ignorant of the worldly affairs | | 18-26-201 | |

One who is not able to stop the following of thoughts and considerations
For them the mind seeks for total rest | | 18-27-202 | |

Without any concentration of mind, or without any distraction
The mind does not aspire for liberation or thinks of bondage | | 18-28-203 | |

From within, one who has self pride and ego
Even when not acting, ACTS | | 18-29-204 | |

Either ways - neither in trouble nor with satisfied smile
The mind is always actionless | | 18-30-205 | |

After acting upon directionless goals
There is no meditative mind | | 18-31-206 | |

After understanding the meaning of the real elements of truth
Even a stupid person is bewildered | | 18-32-207 | |

Practicing meditation and stopping of thoughts
That is what stupid people try to do | | 18-33-208 | |

Even without trying or with lots of efforts
The stupid people do not attain cessation from thoughts | | 18-34-209 | |

Your practices to be pious, intelligent, lovable, perfect
Without worrying, put all of them at total rest || 18-35-210 ||

Even after deliberate thoughtful actions, liberation will not be achieved by...
Stupid who keeps repeating the lessons || 18-36-211 ||

Stupid even after deliberate thoughtfulness will not achieve the ultimate
Even if they wish the same - birth after birth || 18-37-212 ||

Like a person without any support, or eager to find some fate
The stupid will wear every attire given by society || 18-38-213 ||

When one does not attain and benefit from peace
Then the stupid wishes of controlling his and other's mind || 18-39-214 ||

Non-living things, when one worships
How can there be real witnessing? || 18-40-215 ||

One who is trying to control the self & mind is the most stupid
Actually one has to open up the self and mind || 18-41-216 ||

When one shows emotional behavior for sake of showing
Those can never do any help to anyone, anytime || 18-42-217 ||

Those who consider their behavior as of pure non-dual self / soul
They do not know that they are suffering from delusion || 18-43-218 ||

Achieving liberation with the help of one's mind
Those knowledge will never be attain in inner self || 18-44-219 ||

Whenever they come across subjects as scary like tigers
They get shocked and surrender themselves to the subject || 18-45-220 ||

Without any desires, if you are able to see the Almighty
Then you will not take interest in any subjects || 18-46-221 ||

One's mind that does not think about getting liberated
Those people are without any elements of doubts || 18-47-222 ||

Just by listening to things around you
You will have calm pure knowledge within you || 18-48-223 ||

Whatever appears in front of a person to be done
Be a person who immediately without delay does that || 18-49-224 ||

By inner freedom, one attains happiness
Through freedom one attains the highest being || 18-50-225 ||

When one realizes that one is neither a doer nor an enjoyer
The state of believing in self is destroyed || 18-51-226 ||

The actions those are without motive and pretentious
Those people rule and shine in all types of situations || 18-52-227 ||

Those are stupid ones who can enjoy midst many comforts
And retire off to the mountain caves | | 18-53-228 | |

One honors everyone equally
- Warriors, Gods, holy places, kings, or beloved | | 18-54-229 | |

Nor feels humiliated by - Servants, sons,
wives, daughters, grandchildren, relatives and friends | | 18-55-230 | |

Even when pleased, one is not pleased
Even when in pain, one is not suffering in pain | | 18-56-231 | |

Don't have this burden of duty to achieve something in the world
So you would not have anything to regret for every morning | | 18-57-232 | |

Even while doing nothing - one is distracted
Those are the stupid ones who remain agitated every time | | 18-58-233 | |

One sits happily, one sleeps happily
And lives the life of illusion in happiness | | 18-59-234 | |

One who has realized one's own self does not feel distressed
Just like ordinary people, even in their daily practical dealings | | 18-60-235 | |

For stupid ones who retire and try to remain inactive
Automatically generate activities | | 18-61-236 | |

The attempts from liberation from every other worldly thing
That is the only thing that a fool sees | | 18-62-237 | |

'To think' or 'not to think',
The vision of a fool is always caught in those thoughts | | 18-63-238 | |

Whatever works one starts without any desires
Those are the seers like godly child | | 18-64-239 | |

Blessed is one who knows one's self
And shows equality in all types of emotions | | 18-65-240 | |

Where is the world? Where are the illusions?
Where is the end? Where are the tools and means? | | 18-66-241 | |

By one's own self, the one who 'let goes' victories is a sage
That is the one who has completely abandoned self goals | | 18-67-242 | |

Without saying anything more, who is free from elements of knowledge
Is the one who is the great soul | | 18-68-243 | |

All the world phenomenon and knowledge
It is just by name, that they are manifested and differentiated | | 18-69-244 | |

Everything is clouded within the spectrum of illusion
Certainly, there are NO things that really exists | | 18-70-245 | |

What is the use of having pure, energetic, radiant self
After one has achieved the sense of witnessing one's emotions? || 18-71-246 ||

One who is acquired limitless energy radiance within one's own nature
There is nothing to be achieved further || 18-72-247 ||

Until the world reaches this self-realization
Only illusions will persist || 18-73-248 ||

When one is limitless, imperishable and beyond pain
Only after realizing that, one becomes a seer || 18-74-249 ||

When one starts the activities to stop thoughts
Then starts the attitude of stubbornness || 18-75-250 ||

Even after hearing the truth, the one who is not able to leave other worldly things
Those are ones who are really stupid || 18-76-251 ||

With the dawn of knowledge even after those who have ceased to be active
For ordinary person, they will still be considered active || 18-77-252 ||

Where is the darkness? Where is the light?
Where is harming anyone? Where is anything around? || 18-78-253 ||

Where is patience? Where is courtesy?
And where there is fearlessness? || 18-79-254 ||

There is no heaven. There is no hell.
Nor there is any liberation during this life. || 18-80-255 ||

Nor does one longs & yearns for any benefits
Nor one thinks of why one is not benefited || 18-81-256 ||

Nor does one praise the peace and calmness
Nor does one blames the wicked, cheaters & liars || 18-82-257 ||

Nor does one attempt to attain the world within one self
Nor does have any other types of goals in life || 18-83-258 ||

Without hope for compassion, or expectations from children or wife
Without any desire of any activities from any subjects || 18-84-259 ||

Peace and contentment is everywhere for those ones
Who lives steadily despite whatever happens to oneself || 18-85-260 ||

Let the body undergo the cycles of birth and death
The great souls do not at all worry about those things || 18-86-261 ||

Without any possessions and things, without worrying of work and activity
Those are the one stands alone without any duality or desires || 18-87-262 ||

The earth and its dazzles are the same
Those are the ones are devoid of the thing called 'self' || 18-88-263 ||

One who does not want to compare oneself with everyone around
Those are the ones who have no desire for anything || 18-89-264 ||

One who does not want to knows even after knowing
The one who knows what to say but does not say || 18-90-265 ||

A beggar or even the king of everyone
Who is without any attachment to activity – excels and shines || 18-91-266 ||

Where is self-cleansing virtuous behavior? Where is hesitation in doing things?
Where is any certainty of things around you? || 18-92-267 ||

One who is content, restful, peaceful within one's own self
Remains free from pain and discontentment || 18-93-268 ||

Even while in deep sleep one is not asleep
And does not even lie down while dreaming || 18-94-269 ||

Certainly, the one is without thoughts, even in self-generating thoughts
Or is devoid of sense, even after having all sense in one's body || 18-95-270 ||

That one is not happy, or sad with you
Nor the one is detached, or attached with you || 18-96-271 ||

The one is not distracted in distractions
In meditation, one is not meditating || 18-97-272 ||

The liberated one is healthy and fine under all circumstances
And is free from the duty of "I have done" or "I have still to do" || 18-98-273 ||

The one is not pleased when praised as knowledgeable
Nor angry when one does not consider one with knowledge || 18-99-274 ||

Those ones do not run away to find peace to popular worship places
Nor they go to peaceful solitude wilderness || 18-100-275 ||

JANAK SEEKS PEACE IN SOUL

|| **Chapter Nineteen** ||

Janaka said ||

The whole elementary knowledge and lesson
Has gone deep into the recesses of my heart || 19-1-176 ||

Where is religious duty? And where is need to do any work?
Where is desire for meanings? And where is courtesy and manners? || 19-2-177 ||

Where there was past? Where there is future?
Even where there is even the present? || 19-3-178 ||

Where is self soul? Where is non-self?
Where is auspicious? Or where is even in-auspicious? || 19-4-179 ||

Where is the dream? Where is the sleep?
Even where is the state of being awake? || 19-5-180 ||

Where is the farness? Where is the nearness?
Neither – where is the universe or the inner soul? || 19-6-181 ||

Even where is the death & birth? Where are the worldly things?
And where are the worldly attachments and relationships? || 19-7-182 ||

Remember, there is no need to talk of three goals of life,
Even there is no need to converse on Yoga and its benefit. || 19-8-183 ||

JANAK'S REALIZATION OF LIFE

|| Chapter Twenty ||

Janaka said | |

Where is the being? Where is the body?
Where are the central senses of the body? Or even where is mind? | | 20-1-184 | |

Where are the scriptures? Where is the science of knowing self and soul?
Where is the mind that is free from the objects and subjects around it? | | 20-2-185 | |

Where is knowledge? Where is ignorance?
Where is I? Where is this? Where is mine? | | 20-3-186 | |

Where is past life's lasting karma?
Where is even the thought of liberation from this life? | | 20-4-187 | |

Where is the 'doer'? Even where is the one 'reaper'?
Even where is the incessant universal energy? | | 20-5-188 | |

Where is the universe? Where are seekers of liberation?
Where is seeker of path of life? Where is one who is knowledgeable? | | 20-6-189 | |

Where is the creation? And where is destruction?
Where is the end of everything? Where are the means to the end? | | 20-7-190 | |

Where is the proof of the universal soul?
Where is love? Where is enlightenment? | | 20-8-191 | |

Where there is hindrance? Where there is meditative concentration?
Where there is lack of understanding? Where is there stupidity? | | 20-9-192 | |

Where there is deliberate maintaining of relationship?
Where is there truth or absolute truth? | | 20-10-193 | |

Where is there illusion? Where is the world?
Even where is the love's attachment and detachment? | | 20-11-194 | |

What is remaining active? What is retirement?
Where there is freedom? Where there is bondage? | | 20-12-195 | |

Where are the lessons and teachings? Where are the scriptures?
Where is the disciple? Even where is the teacher? | | 20-13-196 | |

Where there is existence? Even where there is non-existence?
What more is there to say? Where is the duality? | | 20-14-197 | |

|| That's the only truth||

Printed in Great Britain
by Amazon

28024861R00037